MIRACLES &
DEDICATION

*Christian Devotions for
the Festival of Lights*

Leah Lesesne, MA

Scripture quotations are from the versions below as denoted by their initials:

New American Standard Bible (NASB)

Copyright © 1960, 1962, 1963, 1968, 1971, 1972, 1973, 1975, 1977, 1995 by The Lockman Foundation

New International Version (NIV)

Holy Bible, New International Version®, NIV® Copyright ©1973, 1978, 1984, 2011 by Biblica, Inc.® Used by permission. All rights reserved worldwide.

Holman Christian Standard Bible (HCSB)

Table of Contents

Introduction

A Brief History of Hanukkah

At its core, Hanukkah is a celebration of the miraculous. In 168 B.C. Jerusalem was occupied by Syrians who desecrated the temple and set up idols of worship for Greek gods. The Jews came under extreme persecution, given the options of death or religious conversion. The head priest at the time was Mattathias, and his son Judah Maccabee became a leader among the Jewish people in resisting the Syrian army. The story of their revolt and the miracle of Hanukkah can be found in 1st and 2nd Maccabees[1], Apocryphal books that hold historical significance.

Despite extreme disadvantages, Judah Maccabee and his revolters were successful against the Syrians and after winning two major battles reclaimed control of the temple. After they removed the desecrations from the temple, they wanted to rededicate the temple to YHWH as soon as possible. But there was one problem, they did not have enough oil to keep the lampstand burning continuously. They only had enough for one night. The rituals to purify oneself for making the oil took seven days and then an additional day actually to make the oil. God had commanded that the lampstand always be burning, but they did not have enough to last the eight days needed to purify more oil.

Rather than dishonoring the process God had instructed them to follow, in their passion to light the lampstand immediately, they took a leap of faith and lit it with the little purified oil they had. Miraculously the lampstand continued to burn for an additional seven nights, long enough for them to ritually purify themselves and make more purified oil.

The Jews in Maccabee's day had not heard from God in hundreds of years. There had been no prophets, no miracles, and there would not be for over another hundred years when John the Baptist prepared the way for Jesus the Messiah. Out of these 400 years of silence[2] came a miracle of light, prophetically symbolizing The Light of the World yet to come.

Hanukkah in Scripture

In scripture we see it Hanukkah referred to in John 10:22 as the Feast of Dedication. Jesus celebrated Hanukkah, though not the way we think of today with menorahs, dreidels, and gifts. In his day it was a celebration both of God's miraculous provision and the dedication of the temple. In the new covenant we are the temple, and this is a beautiful season to rededicate the whole of our lives to God as we thank him for the miracles we have seen in our own lives and partner with him expectantly for even greater miracles.

Though modern Hanukkah traditions have evolved to include gifts and culturally resemble more of a Christmas type celebration focused on family gatherings, the readings and blessings used at Hanukkah are not a modern addition. These are the same readings Jesus observed in celebrating the Feast of Dedication. The schedule of Torah readings has been around for centuries. Which is why it is so significant when Jesus was handed the scroll in Luke 4 that he read Isaiah 61, declaring it was about himself. He had not just chosen that reading; it was the scheduled reading for that day.

The Hanukkah readings are significant because the original tabernacle was dedicated on the 25th of the Hebrew month Kislev, the same date a thousand years later that the Maccabee priests found themselves rededicating the second temple. Centuries before Hanukkah existed, the reading schedule already had passages about the dedication of the tabernacle established for this time. (For more on the Hebrew calendar and holidays check out my other book *Healing in the Hebrew Months: A Biblical Understanding of Each Season's Emotional Healing*.)

Celebrating Hanukkah as a Christian

As Christians we are of course free to celebrate or not celebrate Hanukkah and other Old Testament holidays as we see fit. Paul made clear that as Christ followers we are not bound by Jewish religious tradition and do not need to become Jewish to follow Jesus (Galatians 2, Acts 15). So why celebrate Hanukkah at all?

Throughout scripture, the holidays Israel celebrated were prophetic symbols pointing to Jesus. Yom Kippur, the Day of Atonement, prophesies the final atonement Jesus made for us on the cross. Passover prophesies how his blood covers over our sins. While Hanukkah is not an Old Testament holiday, it is a prophetic symbol of The Light of World shining in the darkness.

As Christians we can celebrate the miraculous provision prophesied in Hanukkah. The Maccabees honored God's commands by not using impure oil for the lamps, and he provided the needed oil to keep the lamp burning. Much like God provided a ram for Abraham to sacrifice instead of Isaac (Genesis 22).

In 2 Kings 4:1-7 we see another time that God miraculously multiplied oil. This time it was not purified oil, but oil of provision for a widow and her sons. Elisha told the woman to gather as many jars as she could find, pour the little oil she had into the jars, and then sell the oil to pay her debts and provide for her family. God's provision doesn't always come the way we'd like or expect, but he is faithful to provide in both natural and miraculous ways.

In Matthew 25 we see another example of oil and a lamp that must be kept burning. Jesus tells the parable of the ten virgins and the oil they needed to keep their wicks lit as they waited for their beloved's return. Five of them were wise and brought extra oil to keep their lamps burning. But five of them were foolish and when their beloved returned, they were not there to meet him because they had gone to buy more oil.

Hanukkah is a perfect picture of this parable and the need to keep our lights burning. Thankfully, Jesus has already supplied all the oil we need through the Holy Spirit who dwells within us. The miracle of Hanukkah is not celebrated simply because of the provision of multiplied oil, but because of the significance that oil held in the dedication of the temple. We no longer go to a physical temple to meet with God, but instead we are his temple. The word Hanukkah means dedication, as the Jews ritually purified themselves to make the oil during the first Hanukkah, this season is a wonderful time to renew our personal dedication to God and get a fresh baptism of the Holy Spirit.

Lighting Candles

The miracle of Hanukkah and its celebration begin with light, a foreshadowing of the Light who came not even 200 years after the Maccabees lit the lampstand in faith. And John begins his gospel with the language of light to describe Jesus:

> "In the beginning was the Word,
> and the Word was with God,
> and the Word was God.
> He was with God in the beginning.
> All things were created through Him,
> and apart from Him not one thing was created
> that has been created.
> Life was in Him,

and that life was the light of men.

That light shines in the darkness,

yet the darkness did not overcome it.

There was a man named John [the Baptist]

who was sent from God.

He came as a witness

to testify about the light,

so that all might believe through him.

He was not the light,

but he came to testify about the light.

The true light, who gives light to everyone,

was coming into the world."

John 1:1-9 (HCSB)

While we often think of Jesus as the Light of the World, he also refers to us that way, as we shine his light within us:

"You are the light of the world. A city situated on a hill cannot be hidden. No one lights a lamp and puts it under a basket, but rather on a lampstand, and it gives light for all who are in the house. In the same way, let your light shine before men, so that they may see your good works and give glory to your Father in heaven"

Matthew 5:14-16 (HCSB).

As you light the candles, take time to notice how the darkness flees. Maybe turn off all the other lights in the room and let your eyes adjust to only the candle light. Do the candles illuminate the room better when placed higher or lower? What happens if you block the light with another object? Recall these verses each night when the candles are lit, The Light of the World, and the light he's placed inside of you.

Traditionally the candles are placed on the menorah from right to left, and then lit from left to right. The middle candle which is typically taller than the rest, is called the shammash, or servant candle. It remains lit throughout Hanukkah and is used to light the other candles each night. Jesus is our shammash. He did not come to be served, but to serve (Mark 10:45). The shammash candle is a beautiful picture of The Light of the World, serving to give light to each of us.

A menorah is typically used to celebrate Hanukkah and mark each night, but any candle or candles you have on hand will work. Maybe pick one candle to be your shammash and keep it lit each night, using it to light your other candles.

Modern Liturgy

Hanukkah is often celebrated by lighting the candles, saying some blessings, and reading from the Torah. The standard Jewish blessings and Torah portions are linked in the reference section.[3,4] The blessings and readings here are modeled after the traditional ones, but also include blessings adapted to fit a Christian perspective and readings from a portion of the traditional Jewish schedule as well as New Testament portions.

If you're unfamiliar with liturgy, the blessings may feel a bit awkward at first. Think of them like worship lyrics or a declaration that you can affirm by reading out loud or pondering in your heart. After the blessings and readings, there is a reflection section to go deeper with what you've read, and a sample prayer to engage with the night's material. Don't let the prayers just be something you read and call done. Take the example prayer and make it your own, go deeper with what God is saying to you specifically that night.

In most years, Hanukkah falls before Christmas on the calendar. Let this celebration prepare your heart for a Christmas focused on Christ.

Night One

Blessings

Blessed are You, Lord our God, King of the Universe, who gave us the gift of salvation through Jesus' death and resurrection. We light these candles as a reminder of the Light of the World.

Blessed are You, Lord our God, King of the Universe, the miracle working God, who promises we will do even greater things by the power of your Spirit. We dedicate our whole lives to you.

Blessed are You, Lord our God, King of the universe, by whom we take our every breath, who meets our every need, and who delights to fulfill the desires of our hearts.

Readings

"Now on the day that Moses had finished setting up the tabernacle, he anointed it and consecrated it with all its furnishings and the altar and all its utensils; he anointed them and consecrated them also. Then the leaders of Israel, the heads of their fathers' households, made an offering (they were the leaders of the tribes; they were the ones who were over the numbered men). When they brought their offering before the Lord, six covered carts and twelve oxen, a cart for every two of the leaders and an ox for each one, then they presented them before the tabernacle.

Then the Lord spoke to Moses, saying, "Accept these things from them, that they may be used in the service of the tent of meeting, and you shall give them to the Levites, to each man according to his service." So Moses took the carts and the oxen and gave them to the Levites. Two carts and four oxen he gave to the sons of Gershon, according to their service, and four carts and eight oxen he gave to the sons of Merari, according to their service, under the direction of Ithamar the son of Aaron the priest. But he did not give any to the sons of Kohath because theirs was the service of the holy objects, which they carried on the shoulder.

The leaders offered the dedication offering for the altar when it was anointed, so the leaders offered their offering before the altar. Then the Lord said to Moses, "Let them present their offering, one leader each day, for the dedication of the altar."

Now the one who presented his offering on the first day was Nahshon the son of Amminadab, of the tribe of Judah; and his offering was one silver dish whose weight was one hundred and thirty shekels, one silver bowl of seventy shekels, according to the shekel of the sanctuary, both of them full of fine flour mixed with oil for a grain offering; one gold pan of ten shekels, full of incense; one bull, one ram, one male lamb one year old, for a burnt offering; one male goat for a sin offering; and for the sacrifice of peace offerings, two oxen, five rams, five male goats, five male lambs one year old. This was the offering of Nahshon the son of Amminadab."

Numbers 7:1-17 (NASB)

"Therefore, brothers, by the mercies of God, I urge you to present your bodies as a living sacrifice, holy and pleasing to God; this is your spiritual worship."

Romans 12:1 (HCSB)

Reflection

Dedication in the old covenant required the continual shedding of blood. Now in the new covenant we are forever covered by Jesus' blood.

What do the elaborate steps in this passage tell us about God's heart for connection with us?

Why is dedication still important in the new covenant?

What does it look like to offer your body as a living sacrifice?

Prayer

Jesus, thank you for your body broken for me, your blood poured out.

Teach me what it means to daily give my body as a living sacrifice. I want to live every day dedicated to you and your Kingdom.

Night Two

Blessings

Blessed are You, Lord our God, King of the Universe, who gave us the gift of salvation through Jesus' death and resurrection. We light these candles as a reminder of the Light of the World.

Blessed are You, Lord our God, King of the Universe, the miracle working God, who promises we will do even greater things by the power of your Spirit. We dedicate our whole lives to you.

Readings

"On the second day Nethanel son of Zuar, leader of Issachar, presented an offering. As his offering, he presented one silver dish weighing 3¼ pounds and one silver basin weighing 1¾ pounds, measured by the standard sanctuary shekel, both of them full of fine flour mixed with oil for a grain offering; one gold bowl weighing four ounces, full of incense; one young bull, one ram, and one male lamb a year old, for a burnt offering; one male goat for a sin offering; and two bulls, five rams, five male breeding goats, and five male lambs a year old, for the fellowship sacrifice. This was the offering of Nethanel son of Zuar."

Numbers 7:18-23 (HCSB)

"Don't you believe that the Father is living in me and that I am living in the Father? Even my words are not my own but come from my Father, for he lives in me and performs his miracles of power through me. Believe that I live as one with my Father and that my Father lives as one with me—or at least, believe because of the mighty miracles I have done.

I tell you this timeless truth: The person who follows me in faith, believing in me, will do the same mighty miracles that I do—even greater miracles than these because I go to be with my Father! For I will do whatever you ask me to do when you ask me in my name. And that is how the Son will show what the Father is really like and bring glory to him. Ask me anything in my name, and I will do it for you!

Loving me empowers you to obey my commands. And I will ask the Father and he will give you another Savior, the Holy Spirit of Truth, who will be to you a friend just like me—and he will never leave you. The world won't receive him because they can't see him or know him. But you will know him intimately, because he will make his home in you and will live inside you."

John 14:10-17 (TPT)

Reflection

When was the last time you saw a miracle, big or small?

What did that miracle teach you about God's heart?

Are there miracles you are still waiting for? Times when you needed a miracle, and it didn't happen?

Should our beliefs about God's heart towards us change based on if we see a miracle or not?

Prayer

Father God, it hurts and is so confusing when I don't see the miracles you've promised.

Help me to stand firm in my belief that you are good, that your heart towards me is loving, and that your desire is always to heal.

Night Two

Miracles & Dedication

Night Three

Blessings

Blessed are You, Lord our God, King of the Universe, who gave us the gift of salvation through Jesus' death and resurrection. We light these candles as a reminder of the Light of the World.

Blessed are You, Lord our God, King of the Universe, the miracle working God, who promises we will do even greater things by the power of your Spirit. We dedicate our whole lives to you.

Readings

"On the third day, Eliab son of Helon, the leader of the people of Zebulun, brought his offering. His offering was one silver plate weighing a hundred and thirty shekels and one silver sprinkling bowl weighing seventy shekels, both according to the sanctuary shekel, each filled with the finest flour mixed with olive oil as a grain offering; one gold dish weighing ten shekels, filled with incense; one young bull, one ram and one male lamb a year old for a burnt offering; one male goat for a sin offering; and two oxen, five rams, five male goats and five male lambs a year old to be sacrificed as a fellowship offering. This was the offering of Eliab son of Helon."

Numbers 7:24-29 (NIV)

"Loving me empowers you to obey my word. And my Father will love you so deeply that we will come to you and make you our dwelling place. But those who don't love me will not obey my words. The Father did not send me to speak my own revelation, but the words of my Father. I am telling you this while I am still with you. But when the Father sends the Spirit of Holiness, the One like me who sets you free, he will teach you all things in my name. And he will inspire you to remember every word that I've told you.

I leave the gift of peace with you—my peace. Not the kind of fragile peace given by the world, but my perfect peace. Don't yield to fear or be troubled in your hearts—instead, be courageous!"

John 14:23-27 (TPT)

"Empower us, as your servants, to speak the word of God freely and courageously. Stretch out your hand of power through us to heal, and to move in signs and wonders by the name of your holy Son, Jesus!" At that moment the earth shook beneath them, causing the building they were in to tremble. Each one of them was filled with the Holy Spirit, and they proclaimed the word of God with unrestrained boldness.

All the believers were one in mind and heart. Selfishness was not a part of their community, for they shared everything they had with one another. The apostles gave powerful testimonies about the resurrection of the Lord Jesus, and great measures of grace rested upon them all. Some who owned houses or land sold them and brought the proceeds before the apostles to distribute to those without. Not a single person among them was needy."

Acts 4:29-35 (TPT)

Reflection

What does love empower us to do?

How does your life reflect the powerful Love living within you?

What happens when believers come together in one mind and heart?

Prayer

Jesus, remind me again how much you love me. Soften any place that has grown hard to your love.

I dedicate my heart to you; Holy Spirit come and fill me even more. Teach me what it means to live empowered.

Bring unity to the believers in my family, my church, my city, so we see the miraculous power of being in one mind and heart - filled with the grace and the gospel, that none may be needy in body, mind, or spirit.

Night Four

Blessings

Blessed are You, Lord our God, King of the Universe, who gave us the gift of salvation through Jesus' death and resurrection. We light these candles as a reminder of the Light of the World.

Blessed are You, Lord our God, King of the Universe, the miracle working God, who promises we will do even greater things by the power of your Spirit. We dedicate our whole lives to you.

Readings

"On the fourth day Elizur the son of Shedeur, the chief of the people of Reuben: his offering was one silver plate whose weight was 130 shekels, one silver basin of 70 shekels, according to the shekel of the sanctuary, both of them full of fine flour mixed with oil for a grain offering; one golden dish of 10 shekels, full of incense; one bull from the herd, one ram, one male lamb a year old, for a burnt offering; one male goat for a sin offering; and for the sacrifice of peace offerings, two oxen, five rams, five male goats, and five male lambs a year old. This was the offering of Elizur the son of Shedeur."

Numbers 7:30-35 (ESV)

"And he said to them, 'As you go into all the world, preach openly the wonderful news of the gospel to the entire human race! Whoever believes the good news and is baptized will be saved, and whoever does not believe the good news will be condemned. And these miracle signs will accompany those who believe: They will drive out demons in the power of my name. They will speak in tongues. They will be supernaturally *overcome their enemies and attacks on their character.* And they will lay hands on the sick and heal them.'

After saying these things, Jesus was lifted up into heaven and sat down at the place of honor at the right hand of God! And the apostles went out announcing the good news everywhere, as the Lord himself consistently worked with them, validating the message they preached with miracle-signs that accompanied them!"

Mark 16: 15-19 (TPT)

Italics paraphrased from TPT footnotes

"For seven days you shall prepare daily a goat for a sin offering; also a young bull and a ram from the flock, without blemish, shall be prepared. For seven days they shall make atonement for the altar and purify it; so shall they consecrate it. When they have completed the days, it shall be that on the eighth day and onward, the priests shall offer your burnt offerings on the altar, and your peace offerings; and I will accept you,' declares the Lord God."

Ezekiel 43:25-27 (NASB)

Reflection

How do we gain acceptance with God in the old and new covenants?

Why are miracle signs an important symbol of our belief?

What is the connection between evangelism and miracles?

Prayer

God, I'm sorry for all the times I've tried to gain your acceptance with what I do. Thank you for accepting me simply because of Jesus and my belief in him.

Expand my belief for the miracle signs I haven't seen yet. Fill me with boldness for the gospel and give me your eyes to see people the way you see them.

Night Four

Night Five

Blessings

Blessed are You, Lord our God, King of the Universe, who gave us the gift of salvation through Jesus' death and resurrection. We light these candles as a reminder of the Light of the World.

Blessed are You, Lord our God, King of the Universe, the miracle working God, who promises we will do even greater things by the power of your Spirit. We dedicate our whole lives to you.

Readings

"On the fifth day it was Shelumiel the son of Zurishaddai, leader of the children of Simeon; his offering was one silver dish whose weight was one hundred and thirty shekels, one silver bowl of seventy shekels, according to the shekel of the sanctuary, both of them full of fine flour mixed with oil for a grain offering; one gold pan of ten shekels, full of incense; one bull, one ram, one male lamb one year old, for a burnt offering; one male goat for a sin offering; and for the sacrifice of peace offerings, two oxen, five rams, five male goats, five male lambs one year old. This was the offering of Shelumiel the son of Zurishaddai."

Numbers 7:36-41 (NASB)

"So all of this magnifies the truth that we have a superior covenant with God than what they experienced, for Jesus himself is its guarantor! As additional proof, we know there were many priests under the old system, for they eventually died and their office had to be filled by another. But Jesus permanently holds his priestly office, since he lives forever and will never have a successor! So he is able to save fully from now throughout eternity, everyone who comes to God through him, because he lives to pray continually for them. He is the High Priest who perfectly fits our need—holy, without a trace of evil, without the ability to deceive, incapable of sin, and exalted beyond the heavens! Unlike the former high priests, he is not compelled to offer daily sacrifices. They had to bring a sacrifice first for their own sins, then for the sins of the people, but he finished the sacrificial system, once and for all, when he offered himself. The law appointed flawed men as high priests, but God's promise, sealed with his oath, which succeeded the law, appoints a perfect Son who is complete forever!"

Hebrews 7:22-27 (TPT)

Reflection

Can you imagine having to give offerings continually like the Israelites did?

Are there ways you fall back into an offerings (or works based) mindset with your salvation?

What would it look like to give up those mindsets and truly rest in Jesus alone for your salvation?

Prayer

Jesus, thank you for being my high priest and bringing an end to the sacrificial system.

Set me free from the mindsets that keep me trapped in works-based lies.

Give me a greater understanding of what it means that you pray for me continually.

Night Five

Miracles & Dedication

Night Six

Blessings

Blessed are You, Lord our God, King of the Universe, who gave us the gift of salvation through Jesus' death and resurrection. We light these candles as a reminder of the Light of the World.

Blessed are You, Lord our God, King of the Universe, the miracle working God, who promises we will do even greater things by the power of your Spirit. We dedicate our whole lives to you.

Readings

"On the sixth day Eliasaph son of Deuel, the leader of the people of Gad, brought his offering. His offering was one silver plate weighing a hundred and thirty shekels and one silver sprinkling bowl weighing seventy shekels, both according to the sanctuary shekel, each filled with the finest flour mixed with olive oil as a grain offering; one gold dish weighing ten shekels, filled with incense; one young bull, one ram and one male lamb a year old for a burnt offering; one male goat for a sin offering; and two oxen, five rams, five male goats and five male lambs a year old to be sacrificed as a fellowship offering. This was the offering of Eliasaph son of Deuel."

Numbers 7:42-47 (HCSB)

"This is what Yahweh says: "The heavens are my throne and the earth is my footstool. Where is the house you will build for me? Where is the place where I will rest? My hand made these things so they all belong to me," declares Yahweh. "But there is one my eyes are drawn to: the humble one, the tender one, the trembling one who lives in awe of all I say.""

Isaiah 66:1-2 (TPT)

"So if our sins have been forgiven and forgotten, why would we ever need to offer another sacrifice for sin? And now we are brothers and sisters in God's family because of the blood of Jesus, and he welcomes us to come right into the most holy sanctuary in the heavenly realm—boldly and with no hesitation. For he has dedicated a new, life-giving way for us to approach God. For just as the veil was torn in two, Jesus' body was torn open to give us free and fresh access to him! And since we now have a magnificent King-Priest to welcome us into God's house, we come closer to God and approach him with an open heart, fully convinced by faith that nothing will keep us at a distance from him. For our hearts have been sprinkled with blood to remove impurity and we have been freed from an accusing conscience and now we are clean, unstained, and presentable to God inside and out!"

Hebrews 10:18-22 (TPT)

Reflection

The God of the universe, who created all things, chooses to make his home in you. What does this say about how God feels about you?

What would it look like to live fully aware of the free access you have to God?

Where do you need more boldness in your relationship with God?

Prayer

Holy Spirit, thank you for making your home in me. Awaken me to a full awareness of your presence and of your voice continually speaking to me.

Fill me with boldness to approach you without fear.

Night Six

Night Seven

Blessings

Blessed are You, Lord our God, King of the Universe, who gave us the gift of salvation through Jesus' death and resurrection. We light these candles as a reminder of the Light of the World.

Blessed are You, Lord our God, King of the Universe, the miracle working God, who promises we will do even greater things by the power of your Spirit. We dedicate our whole lives to you.

Readings

"On the seventh day Elishama the son of Ammihud, the chief of the people of Ephraim: his offering was one silver plate whose weight was 130 shekels, one silver basin of 70 shekels, according to the shekel of the sanctuary, both of them full of fine flour mixed with oil for a grain offering; one golden dish of 10 shekels, full of incense; one bull from the herd, one ram, one male lamb a year old, for a burnt offering; one male goat for a sin offering; and for the sacrifice of peace offerings, two oxen, five rams, five male goats, and five male lambs a year old. This was the offering of Elishama the son of Ammihud."

Numbers 7:48-53 (ESV)

"So then, refuse to answer its call to surrender your body as a tool for wickedness. Instead, passionately answer God's call to keep yielding your body to him as one who has now experienced resurrection life! You live now for his pleasure, ready to be used for his noble purpose."

Romans 6:13 (TPT)

"Now my beloved ones, I have saved these most important truths for last: Be supernaturally infused with strength through your life-union with the Lord Jesus. Stand victorious with the force of his explosive power flowing in and through you. Put on God's complete set of armor provided for us, so that you will be protected as you fight against the evil strategies of the accuser!

Your hand-to-hand combat is not with human beings, but with the highest principalities and authorities operating in rebellion under the heavenly realms. For they are a powerful class of demon-god and evil spirits that hold this dark world in bondage. Because of this, you must wear all the armor that God provides so you're protected as you confront the slanderer, for you are destined for all things and will rise victorious.

Put on truth as a belt to strengthen you to stand in triumph. Put on holiness as the protective armor that covers your heart. Stand on your feet alert, then you'll always be ready to share the blessings of peace. In every battle, take faith as your wrap-around shield, for it is able to extinguish the blazing arrows coming at you from the Evil One! Embrace the power of salvation's full deliverance, like a helmet to protect your thoughts from lies. And take the mighty razor-sharp Spirit-sword of the spoken Word of God. Pray passionately in the Spirit, as you constantly intercede with every form of prayer at all times. Pray the blessings of God upon all his believers."

Ephesians 6:10-18 (TPT)

Reflection

What does it look like to yield our bodies to God's purposes?

Why is it important to protect ourselves with armor?

Why is the miraculous important for a spiritual battle?

Prayer

God, thank you for covering me with your armor.

Keep me aware of the real enemy in every situation.

Thank you that you've already won every battle I will ever face.

Night Eight

Blessings

Blessed are You, Lord our God, King of the Universe, who gave us the gift of salvation through Jesus' death and resurrection. We light these candles as a reminder of the Light of the World.

Blessed are You, Lord our God, King of the Universe, the miracle working God, who promises we will do even greater things by the power of your Spirit. We dedicate our whole lives to you.

Readings

"On the eighth day Gamaliel son of Pedahzur, the leader of the people of Manasseh, brought his offering. His offering was one silver plate weighing a hundred and thirty shekels and one silver sprinkling bowl weighing seventy shekels, both according to the sanctuary shekel, each filled with the finest flour mixed with olive oil as a grain offering; one gold dish weighing ten shekels, filled with incense; one young bull, one ram and one male lamb a year old for a burnt offering; one male goat for a sin offering; and two oxen, five rams, five male goats and five male lambs a year old to be sacrificed as a fellowship offering. This was the offering of Gamaliel son of Pedahzur.

(Additional optional reading Numbers 7:60-88)

These were the offerings for the dedication of the altar after it was anointed. When Moses entered the tent of meeting to speak with the Lord, he heard the voice speaking to him from between the two cherubim above the atonement cover on the ark of the covenant law. In this way the Lord spoke to him.

The Lord said to Moses, 'Speak to Aaron and say to him, When you set up the lamps, see that all seven light up the area in front of the lampstand.' Aaron did so; he set up the lamps so that they faced forward on the lampstand, just as the Lord commanded Moses. This is how the lampstand was made: It was made of hammered gold from its base to its blossoms. The lampstand was made exactly like the pattern the Lord had shown Moses."

Numbers 7:54-59, 89; 8:1-4 (NIV)

"When I turned to see the voice that was speaking to me, I saw seven golden lampstands. And walking among the lampstands, I saw someone like a son of man, wearing a full-length robe with a golden sash over his chest. His head and his hair were white like wool—white as glistening snow. And his eyes were like flames of fire! His feet were gleaming like bright metal, as though they were glowing in a fire, and his voice was like the roar of many rushing waters.

In his right hand he held seven stars, and out of his mouth was a sharp, double-edged sword. And his face was shining like the brightness of the blinding sun! When I saw him, I fell down at his feet as good as dead, but he laid his right hand on me and I heard his reassuring voice saying: Don't yield to fear. I am the Beginning and I am the End, the Living One! I was dead, but now look—I am alive forever and ever. And I hold the keys that unlock death and the unseen world."

Revelation 1:12-18 (TPT)

Reflection

If the lampstand was just a part of old covenant offerings, why do you think it's such an important symbol with Jesus in Revelation?

What would it be like to hear God clearly, like Moses did, and to create things with him?

What does the unseen world have to do with miracles?

Prayer

Jesus, you are so glorious! Thank you for revealing yourself as the completion of all sacrifices.

Help me live everyday dedicated to you in body, mind, and spirit.

Teach me what it really means for Holy Spirit to dwell in me and have signs and miracles flow through me.

References

1) 1st and 2nd Maccabees
https://www.biblegateway.com/passage/?search=1+Maccabees+1%3A41-64%2C+2+Maccabees+10%3A1-9&version=NABRE

2) 400 Years of Silence
https://en.wikipedia.org/wiki/Intertestamental_period

https://answersingenesis.org/kids/bible/years-of-silence/

https://zondervanacademic.com/blog/what-happened-between-testaments

3) Traditional Torah Readings
https://www.chabad.org/parshah/torahreading_cdo/aid/3791129/jewish/Text-of-Chanukah-Torah-Readings.htm

4) Traditional Blessings
https://www.chabad.org/holidays/chanukah/article_cdo/aid/103874/jewish/Blessings-on-the-Menorah.htm

Miracles & Dedication

About the Author

Leah Lesesne (pronounced lay-uh luh-sane) delights in connecting with God through the Jewish roots of Christianity and the spiritual rhythms he set in motion. She spent years in the mental health counseling world frustrated by the lack of lasting healing she saw. She knew there had to be better answers for the pain her clients felt. Convinced of God's promise in 1 Thessalonians 5:23 of complete wholeness spirit-mind-body, she returned to her roots of inner healing prayer and found revelation after revelation of God's answers to lasting breakthrough. Her mission is to share those revelations to help you be as healthy, whole, and close to Jesus as possible.

Leah and her family live in Atlanta, GA with their urban farm full of critters. When she's not writing you can find her out in her garden with a good book and a cup of tea, or more likely chasing a wayward chicken.

Find her online:
www.Shelemah.com
www.HealingintheHebrewMonths.com
www.facebook.com/shelemahwellness
www.instagram.com/shelemahwellness

Other Books by Leah

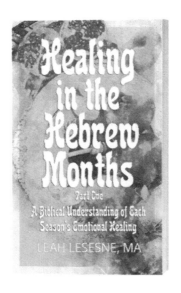

Healing in the Hebrew Months: A Biblical Understanding of Each Season's Emotional Healing

What if you could know what God is doing in each season? Imagine the breakthroughs you'd find if you could synchronize your watch with God's and copy his day-planner. It doesn't take a supernatural revelation of his divine will - it's exactly what's possible for you when you follow the patterns God already laid out in the Hebrew calendar and explore the emotional themes in each month! After all, Ecclesiastes does say there is a time for every purpose under heaven.

Body Coaching: Losing Weight Through Positive Self-Talk

What if you could lose weight just by talking to yourself? What we say to ourselves and about ourselves matters. Body coaching is a 30 day program of positive self-talk. Taking authority in our spirits over our bodies and giving ourselves the pep talks we've desperately needed.

It's not about will powering your way through another diet or exercise program, it's about partnering your body, mind, and spirit together so that you can experience the breakthroughs you've been longing for.

Healthy & Whole: 60 Days to Complete Wellness

Part devotional, part health challenge, Healthy & Whole will take you on a 60-day journey to complete wellness, body-mind-spirit. By building new physical, emotional, and spiritual lifestyles rather than just new habits you will find your unique path to being as healthy, whole, and close to Jesus as possible.

Learn More About the Hebrew Calendar and Holidays

www.HealingintheHebrewMonths.com

Blog posts, books, and other products to help you understand the Hebrew calendar, how it relates to the Biblical narrative, and the spiritual rhythms that still apply to us today. Plus a Facebook group to connect with likeminded believers.

Made in the USA
Coppell, TX
26 November 2022

87102274R00042